INDOOR GARDENING FOR BEGINNERS

Start an Indoor Veggie Garden & Grow Your Vegetables and Herbs at Home

Table Of Contents

Introduction 3

Chapter 1 - Indoor Gardening: An Overview 4

Chapter 2 - Choosing Your Indoor Garden Space 7

Chapter 3 - Indoor Lighting 9

Chapter 5 - Indoor Gardening Tools 15

Chapter 6 - Fertilizers 18

Chapter 7 - The Growing Medium 22

Chapter 8 - Watering 24

Chapter 9 - Hydroponics 26

Chapter 10 - Overview of Growing Indoor Garden Vegetables for Beginners 29

Chapter 11 - Overview of Growing Indoor Garden Herbs for Beginners 32

Chapter 12 - How to Grow Vegetables Indoors ... 35

Chapter 13 - How to Grow Herbs Indoors 48

Chapter 14 - FAQs 57

Conclusion 60

Introduction

I want to thank you and congratulate you for downloading the book, Indoor Gardening for Beginners: Start an Indoor Veggie Garden & Grow Your Vegetables and Herbs at Home.

This book contains proven steps and strategies on how to grow vegetables such as salad greens, potatoes, and carrots as well as herbs such as basil, chives, rosemary and mint right inside your home.

Start a veggie and herb garden indoors and you will realize that you don't really need a large amount of space to enjoy safe, fresh and nutritious produce. This book will tell you all that you need to know to start your very own indoor garden, all the way from the tools, containers, fertilizers, to the steps on how to plant a wide variety of vegetables and herbs. Nothing tastes better than your very own, homegrown crops.

Thanks again for downloading this book; I hope you enjoy it!

Chapter 1 - Indoor Gardening: An Overview

If you want to enjoy freshly picked vegetables and herbs, but you do not have any available space for a garden outdoors, then you will definitely benefit from an indoor garden. Many people have already started growing herbs and veggies successfully inside restricted places such as a sunny corner in their apartment.

Before we move on to the specifics, let us first discuss an overview of what an indoor garden is.

The first thing that you need to do to start your indoor garden is to choose a strategic location inside your home where there is as much sunlight exposure as possible. If there is none or if natural light is insufficient, then you can benefit from artificial lights instead. Finding the right spot will require you to assess the available space. Once you have decided on a particular spot, you can plan out the number of containers as well as their shapes and sizes in order to arrange them strategically and maximize the limited space.

To make your indoor garden a success, you have to keep everything consistent. That means you have to water regularly and at roughly the same time everyday. The lighting your plants receive should be consistent, and the temperature should be stable (approximately 65 to 76F).

The plants that you grow in an indoor garden are the kind that have minimal needs and are suitable to be grown indoors. Choose plants that grow vertically in pots, or hanging plants so as to maximize the available space. Also consider the produce that you will actually be able to use in your home. If you are a busy person, you may want to start your indoor garden with plants that are low maintenance. Some great indoor garden vegetable plant and herb suggestions will be provided in the later part of this book.

After deciding on the types of herbs and vegetables that you would like to grow in your indoor garden, you can now begin to prepare their needs. These would be the types of soil, pebbles, fertilizer and compost.

In an indoor garden, your plants will require more attention because their roots won't be able to go down and search for natural sources of water. In other words, you are their only means of hydration and nutrition. Make yourself a reminder to check your indoor garden from time to time in order to make sure that the soil is moist and that they are receiving sufficient water and sunlight.

Growing your own veggie and herb garden indoors is a fun and rewarding hobby. Mother Nature takes care of the plants outdoors - she gives them sunlight, minerals from the soil, carbon dioxide for their respiration, and water from the sky or underneath the ground. So even though growing plants indoors does require a certain amount of responsibility, you will truly enjoy the results. Now, are you ready to start planning your indoor garden? Let's continue.

Chapter 2 - Choosing Your Indoor Garden Space

In a controlled indoor environment, you will be the provider of most of your plants' needs, so the right location is crucial for your plants to thrive.

In choosing the right space for your plant, avoid areas with too much shade, direct heat, or strong wind. For instance, the windowsill might seem like an ideal spot to start your indoor garden but direct sunlight during the summer will kill them.

Your indoor garden space requires warm and bright light, whether from a natural or artificial source. In most houses, the living room or the dining room can provide this kind of setting. Herbs will do well in the kitchen because they can withstand the fluctuating temperatures and steam in this part of the house. For your seeds and cuttings, pick a cool room in your home with indirect sunlight to give them the ideal environment to germinate.

In assessing the available space for your indoor garden, you should always keep in mind their basic needs: Lighting, Water and Nutrient Sources, and Temperature. You might already have a spot in mind as you are reading this, so if you do you can go ahead and check to see if it will enable you to provide your garden with these four essentials.

Chapter 3 - Indoor Lighting

One of the biggest differences between an outdoor garden and an indoor one is the source of light. Ideally, you should position your indoor garden in an area that allows sufficient (warm, not hot) natural light. However, if your space does not allow this, then you may want to consider artificial lighting. But if you have intermittent natural light, then you can just use indoor lighting whenever it's overcast.

Artificial Indoor Lighting

There are two options for your indoor garden's artificial lighting and these are Fluorescent Lights and High Intensity Discharge or HID.

Fluorescent Lights

Fluorescent lights are often used in nurseries. Because the heat levels are low, they can be positioned just a few inches above your new plants. If you are planning to grow plants that are higher than 10 inches, then you will need a full spectrum fluorescent light bulb.

High Intensity Discharge Lights

High Intensity Discharge lights are more specific for an indoor garden and are used often in greenhouses. They are installed with specific transformers and sockets and operate on a 110/120 volt current (the kind used in the home), but some models can be converted to the 220/240 volt if preferred. Two particular HID light bulbs are used for indoor gardening, and these are the Metal Halide or MH/MS and the High Pressure Sodium or HPS.

Metal Halide Lamps can provide your plants with a balanced light spectrum that can emit blue and red wavelengths ideal for fast plant growth. In other words, it mimics the type of sunlight in the tropics. This means that you can use them to grow your plants right from the start. Just make sure to follow the manufacturer's instructions very carefully for safety reasons.

High Pressure Sodium Lamps provide heavy lighting (30 percent more than the Metal Halide lamp) that is used on plants that require lots of sunlight such as fruit and flowering plants. It has about 10 to 15 percent more lumens per watt compared to a metal halide bulb. You will probably want to invest in a HPS lamp once you are ready to take your indoor garden hobby to the next level.

For a beginner indoor garden, it is best to choose a spot that will provide your plants with as much natural light as possible and to have fluorescent lights or a Metal Halide lamp as an artificial source whenever they are needed.

Chapter 4 - Containers

The key to an efficient plant container is its ability to hold water without soaking the soil nor draining the water so much that it would cause dryness. There are basically two ways for you to house your plants' root system: floor-standing and hanging.

Pots and Baskets for Floor-Standing Plants

Indoor plants are usually grown inside plastic or clay pots. These come in a variety of shapes and sizes, from rectangular to circular. Find a pot that has drainage holes at its base and comes with a matching tray or dish to collect excess water. If you do not like the look of the tray, you can place the pot inside a larger, more decorative container. Just make sure that the brim of the pot does not rise above the decorative container even after you have placed some bricks underneath to keep water from soaking at the bottom.

Other options for Floor-Standing plants would be wicker baskets and metal buckets. Wicker baskets are decorative and can hold your vegetable or herb plant well if it is lined with plastic. Metal containers can be painted to look more aesthetic. To make your indoor garden more inspiring, you can paint your containers with the same color or follow a theme so that your entire garden will look more organized. One recommendation would be to paint all of your containers white and then decorate each container with pictures of their produce. Another suggestion would be to paint the containers to match the rest of the space in order for it to blend in with its indoor environment.

Keep in mind that you do not have to purchase new containers for you to start your indoor garden; simply look around your home for old pots, baskets or any other container that can hold enough soil and house the root system of your plants. Just make sure that the container is one hundred percent waterproof because you do not want to damage your floor whenever you water your garden.

Once you have collected a number of containers for your indoor garden, you can start preparing them by arranging them strategically around your space. After you are satisfied with their arrangement, the next thing to do is to line them with plastic. Then, you place some crockery shards or pebbles on the base to prevent the soil from getting too soaked with water, which will cause the roots to rot.

Hanging Baskets or Wall Pots

Using hanging baskets and wall pots for some of your plants may not be so common indoors, but it is a great option if you have very limited space. A lot of different plants, such as your herbs, will grow very well whether in a hanging or floor-standing basket, as long as you provide a special watering system to help retain moisture and minimize the frequency of watering. One suggestion would be water-retaining gel. In preparing your hanging basket or wall pot, you must first line it with some fiber liner or sphagnum moss to hold the soil before you add the potting soil.

Caring for Your Indoor Containers

Containers usually last for decades, just as long as you check them occasionally to fix any possible damage. If the containers that you are about to use for your indoor garden are old, it is important to scrub them well first to eradicate any pests or viruses.

If you just bought clay pots for your garden, it is recommended that you soak them for 60 minutes in water so that it will not start to soak up the moisture once you start watering your plants. As your clay pots age, green moss will start to grow on it. There is nothing wrong with this, but it is important to ensure that the inside of the pots are cleaned.

If you are planning on using old cans or any other metal container, make sure to line the inside with plastic to separate the metal's minerals from contaminating the potting soil. Wooden containers tend to rot as time goes by, so if you are going to be using them then you will also have to line the insides with plastic. Always create holes at the bottom of your containers for drainage.

Chapter 5 - Indoor Gardening Tools

Tending to your indoor garden will be easier and much more enjoyable when you are equipped with the right tools. Most tools which you will find on the market are actually not "needed", but it does not hurt to have them if you prefer. It is recommended that you purchase the most basic tools first and then slowly build your collection whenever you feel like it.

Basic Indoor Gardening Tools

Caring for your indoor vegetable and herb garden requires the following basic equipment: a gardening trowel, a pair of pruners, a misting spray, a long spout watering can, a dibble, a measuring jug, and a sieve.

The gardening trowel is used to scoop and break up the soil, as well as to aid you in transferring plants from one container to another.

Your pair of pruners will make it easy for you to harvest produce, prune, and propagate your plants.

The misting spray is for you to increase the humidity and water delicate plants.

A watering can with a long spout is the best way to water the roots of your plants by pointing the end of the spout to the soil.

The dibble is for you to create small holes in the potting soil in order to plant your seeds.

The measuring jug will be especially useful for mixing your fertilizers and potting soil.

The sieve is for you to break up lumpy potting soil and thoroughly mix fertilizer with it.

Indoor Nursery Garden Tools

If you are planning to grow your vegetable and herb garden from seeds or cuttings, you will need the dibble along with additional tools: a cell pack or a seed tray, a pencil and some plastic labels, a widger, and a rooting hormone.

You can sow your seeds in the cell pack or the seed tray; the difference between them is that the cell pack takes up more space but will spare you from transplanting the seedlings. Don't forget to label your seedlings.

The widger is to be used when very carefully extracting the seedling from the soil for transplanting. If you are planning to use the rooting hormone, make sure to follow the manufacturer's instructions very carefully.

Staking Tools

Most indoor vegetable plants require staking in order to encourage them to grow in a specific direction, such as tomatoes, bell peppers, and okra. The use of staking tools is highly recommended in order to promote vertical growth and allow the use of minimal space.

While the plant is still young, you will need to occasionally replace the stake in order to keep up with its growth. Some recommendations for staking are split canes or bamboo canes. Use plant rings, green garden string, twine, or garden wire to hold the stems in the right position. Make sure to regularly check your stake to ensure that the rings or wires are not biting into the stem.

Chapter 6 - Fertilizers

Outdoor plants that grow in their natural habitat are well provided for with nutrients and minerals in the soil by drawing them up through a complex root system. In a container, the plant will rely upon you to gain its nutrients daily.

Fertilizers

There are two major types of plant fertilizers and these are organic and inorganic. Organic fertilizers are derived from animal or plant sources, and last longer as the plant tends to soak up its nutrients at a gradual pace. Inorganic fertilizers are mineral-based and usually act faster, which makes it last for a relatively shorter time.

All of your plants will need three main chemical elements for them to grow well, and these are nitrogen for the leaves and shoots, phosphorus for their roots, and potassium for their produce. You will be able to know the amount of each element in your fertilizer by looking at the N:P:K ratio on its packaging. Keep in mind that every plant has a specific requirement when it comes to the different amounts of these elements, along with other elements such as zinc, iron, magnesium, copper and manganese. Research as much as you can on the type of vegetables or herbs that you wish to grow indoors so that you will know their specific required nutrients.

Fertilizers also come in different forms, and these are the slow release granules, slow release pellets, plant spikes, dissolvable crystals, and liquid fertilizer. Make sure to follow the manufacturer's instructions because certain types can be too strong if not properly mixed.

In purchasing a particular fertilizer, you may notice the release rate on the packaging. If it is labeled as "Slow release", it means that the plant will gradually absorb it from 14 to 21 days. If it is "Quick acting", it will last from 7 to 10 days. Liquid fertilizers tend to get absorbed pretty quickly, therefore results can be expected as early as 5 days. Foliar fertilizer lasts for 3 to 4 days; this type of fertilizer is absorbed through the plant's leaves and is ideal for plants that do not really use their root system to draw up nutrients. High potassium fertilizers are ideal for certain vegetables such as tomatoes because they really help in encouraging the growth of flowers and fruit.

The Effects of Too Little Fertilizer

A plant that is not sufficiently fertilized will have stunted growth, and it will look weak and sickly. They are more susceptible to becoming sick or infested by pests. The flowers, leaves and produce, if any, are pale, small, and fall off prematurely.

The Effects of Too Much Fertilizer

Too much fertilizer is also bad for the plants, because it will cause malformations or wilting from absorbing excess amounts of elements. You will also notice the development of white crusts on the top of your soil, and blemishes on the leaves.

The Right Time to Fertilize

Newly potted plants will usually be provided for by the nutrients that are naturally found in the soil. However, once the nutrients are completely drained you will need to add fertilizer. It will depend upon the type of plant as well as the kind of soil as to how long it will take for you to wait until you mix in your fertilizer. Loamy soil, for instance, contains plenty of nutrients and it will take up to 3 months before you start fertilizing the soil. Loamless soil should be fertilized 1 to 2 months after potting. If you bought your plant from a shop then you will need to fertilize it as soon as you pot it because these plants are usually unfed for 14 days to avoid root damage caused by fertilizer build-up.

How to Use Fertilizer

Liquid fertilizer is bought in the form of powder or granules that you will need to dissolve in water, or it is bought as a liquid concentrate. You will be mixing it into the potting soil by using your watering can or a misting spray.

Dry fertilizer is mixed into the potting soil if you are only about to transplant. For old plants you will be placing it on top of the soil and then using some sticks to poke into the soil so as to allow for gradual seepage. Be careful not to let the fertilizer get to the root system because it will damage the roots due to its high concentration of elements.

Chapter 7 - The Growing Medium

A growing medium is the material that provides stability for the plant's root system, helps to balance pH level, and allows sufficient supply of water, air, and nutrients. Your potting soil is a rough example of a growing medium.

Different plants usually require different types of growing media. In indoor gardening, the potting soil needs to be pH neutral (except for plants that require an acidic environment), firm, lightweight, and clean. There are generally two types of soil mix: the loam-based and the loamless.

The loam-based mix contains soil and can hold moisture and nutrients more efficiently compared to the loamless variety. However, they tend to be dense and are thus more appropriate for older and floor-standing plants.

Loamless soil is made of peat or peat-substitute. It is therefore apparently lightweight and easy to handle; however, it tends to dry too quickly and is unable to hold nutrients very well. Some examples, aside from peat, would be coir, moss, coarse sand and silver sand.

Apart from the soil mix, you will also need to add soil additions in order to provide air pockets in the soil for the purpose of boosting drainage. Some examples of soil additions would be perlite, pebbles, crockery shards, vermiculite and charcoal.

In hydroponics (which will be discussed in Chapter 9), the following growing media are recommended: gel, Hydroleca, dry crystals and clay granules.

Chapter 8 - Watering

Your plants will die quickly if they are not watered properly on a regular basis. Plants need the water to bring the nutrients from the soil through the roots across their entire body all the way to the tips of their leaves. Water is responsible for keeping the plant firm and stable, and allows the plant to continue to photosynthesize.

Lack of water will impede or completely stop the plant from functioning. The result will be a wilted, pale and dying plant. Some plants can still recover from wilting, but it is inevitably dead once it has completely browned.

Keep in mind, though, that different plants require different frequencies in watering. Succulent plants require less watering compared to seedlings, for instance, because they are able to retain water for a longer amount of time. The only way for you to know how to properly water a plant is to research its specific needs.

Most vegetable and herb plants require watering from above, meaning you point your long spout watering can directly over the potting soil and pour water. Be careful not to soak the soil but to make sure that there is just enough moisture. Beginner gardeners will greatly benefit from a water indicator tool, which is a special kind of card that you stick into the soil that will change color once the soil becomes dry.

Chapter 9 - Hydroponics

Hydroponics is the process of growing plants without using soil. Instead, a growth medium is used to support the root system. The nutrients are applied directly to the roots. Hydroponics allows watering to become as infrequent as once every 2 or 3 months, making it a convenient option.

Plants that can be grown hydroponically are those which are suited to moist conditions and can tolerate partial shade. Glass is the ideal container for this type of indoor gardening technique.

How to Apply Hydroponics

To illustrate how a plant can be grown hydroponically, let's use the gel medium. The first step is to measure the dry crystals in a container and then to add a specific amount of water based on the manufacturer's instructions.

Upon contact with moisture, the dry crystal will turn into gel. Water is gradually poured onto the gel over an extended period of time to allow it to soak up as much of the moisture as possible. Excess water is drained away.

The plant that will be hydroponically grown should have been rooted in water to allow it to adapt easily to its permanent environment. Once the gel is ready, the plant is transferred to it.

Growing Media

The hydroponic growing medium itself does not provide nutritive value to the plants; all it ever does is to give support to the plant and allow the nutrients from the nutrient solution to be distributed evenly. The growing medium should be non-toxic, sterile, and can retain water and nutrients for a long period of time.

In chapter 7, some of the growing media used in Hydroponics are gel, Hydroleca, dry crystals and clay granules. Apart from these, you can also use the following: rockwool, coconut fiber, fired clay grow rocks, and perlite.

Rockwool is composed of volcanic basaltic rock and a special binder to prevent elements such as potassium hydroxide from percolating into the nutrient solution. It will provide about 90 to 95 percent of air space and 80 percent of nutrient solution. It is known to hold the most nutrient solution among all the growing media.

Coconut fiber or coconut coir is derived from the inner husk of coconuts. It is very water retentive and contains natural rooting hormones.

Fired clay grow rocks, also called fire clay pellets, are produced by submitting clay pellets to extremely high heat. This will cause them to swell up and be filled with air. Fire clay grow rocks can hold plenty of water and air because of their porosity.

Perlite, also known as puffed sand, is lightweight and sterile. It is an ideal growing medium for indoor herbs and vegetables such as cabbage and lettuce. The only problem is that it provides minimal stability to the root system of the plants and sometimes encourages algae growth more often than the other growing media. However, when mixed with clay pellets it works superbly; just make sure to throw it away after first use.

Chapter 10 - Overview of Growing Indoor Garden Vegetables for Beginners

As a beginner to growing vegetables indoors, it is best to know the rule of thumb: your vegetables will need at least 6 to 8 hours of sunlight each day. If you have chosen a spot that gets sunlight from the west and south, then that is great. Otherwise, you will need to install supplemental light fixtures that have full spectrum fluorescent bulbs for your plants.

There are two main types of vegetables that you can grow indoors: the ones that prefer cooler temperatures such as spinach, lettuce, chard and cabbage, and the ones that prefer the warmer temperatures such as beans, tomatoes, cucumbers and peppers. Cool-loving vegetables will thrive in an environment of about 45F, while the heat-loving variety will grow and bear produce in an environment with at least 68F.

The containers for your indoor vegetable garden will depend on the root system of each plant. For example, if you are planning to grow beans, tomatoes, carrots, beets and cucumbers, you will need a deeper container as the root system of these plants is denser. Vegetables such as radishes, lettuce and spinach do not need deep containers, as their roots are only a few inches long. Don't forget to choose only containers that are sturdy and have drainage holes.

Your growing media for cultivating vegetables indoors should be sterile and lightweight, such as peat moss, perlite, sand or vermiculite. Beginners will want to make use of premixes that contain timed-release fertilizer and moisture-retentive crystals, although these can be quite costly.

One of the most important aspects of growing vegetables successfully, whether indoors or outdoors, is to use the right fertilizer. It is highly recommended that you use organic fertilizers such as those derived from fish emulsion and seaweed, although some beginners might find it to be quite tedious to prepare. If you opt for chemical-based fertilizers, you will have specific instructions which you can follow.

Water your indoor vegetable garden regularly. Protect your flooring by placing the containers on top of trays lined with pebbles to prevent the roots from being soaked in water; this will cause molding and root rot. Water the soil just enough for it to feel moist.

One major advantage to indoor gardening is that you will be dealing with much fewer pests. To get rid of spider mites, mealy bugs, white

flies and aphids, you can use
insecticide. Read and follow the manu
instructions carefully so as to av
mishaps.

Below is a list of the most recommended vegetables that you can easily grow indoors as a beginner. All of these vegetables will grow well in a well-draining soil and in an environment with 6 to 8 hours of sunlight.

- Carrots
- Potatoes
- Garlic Greens
- Salad Greens (such as spinach and romaine lettuce)
- Microgreens
- Scallions
- Tomatoes
- Chili Peppers
- Mushrooms

In Chapter 12 of this book, you will be introduced to steps on how to grow each of these delicious vegetables indoors.

Chapter 11 - Overview of Growing Indoor Garden Herbs for Beginners

Growing herbs indoors is a lot more common in households compared to growing vegetables, because they are so easy to cultivate. An indoor herb garden will make the room smell crisp and fragrant, and it will give you access to fresh ingredients for whatever dish you are preparing, anytime.

Your indoor herb garden will require a good soil mix and some stable containers. It needs to be placed in a location that receives plenty of light and has consistent temperature. Many people grow their herbs inside their kitchen, and if you are planning to do that, make sure you place them in an area farthest from sources of fluctuating temperatures, such as the refrigerator and the stove.

Most herbs grow well in sandy growing media that drains very well. You can mix in some compost to the growing media in order to feed your herbs with nutrients. The recommended size for the containers that will house your herbs should be about 8 inches deep, and 6 to 8 inches wide. If you are planning to plant them all in a single, large container, make sure that they are at least 6 inches from each other.

Herbs require at least 5 hours of sunlight every day, even better if it is up to 8 hours. Use fluorescent lighting if you don't have a spot for natural light. Herbs usually need only one or two waterings per week, but this depends on the variety, so it is best to do some research on the particular herb that you wish to grow. Even if watering is not as frequent, your herbs will still need moisture. One common technique is to place the herb pots on top of trays with pebbles and fill the trays with water to give the herbs a moist environment.

Herbs require a special type of fertilizer that is safe for edible plants. Ask your local plant center if they have any available recommendations in your area. Your herb garden needs to be fed with this nutrient source once every 30 days.

One common mistake for most indoor herb gardeners is that they tend to start over-cutting the herbs once they start to flourish. This will kill the plant itself. Be careful not to harvest too much of its leaves so that it will continue to grow and provide you with even more produce.

Below is a list of the most recommended herbs that you can easily grow indoors as a beginner.

- Basil
- Chives

- Cilantro
- Ginger
- Mint
- Rosemary
- Lemongrass
- Oregano
- Parsley

In Chapter 13 of this book, you will be introduced to steps on how to grow each of these fresh herbs indoors.

Chapter 12 - How to Grow Vegetables Indoors

In this chapter, you will be introduced to the different types of vegetables indoors along with the steps on how to grow them successfully.

Carrots

Carrots are one of the healthiest sources of vitamins and minerals, such as vitamins A, B6, C and K, and thiamine, folate, niacin, potassium, manganese and carotenoids.

Steps to Grow Them

To grow carrots, you will need to prepare a container that is at least 18 inches deep and 18 inches wide. You should also ensure that there are drainage holes at its base. Prepare potting soil that is rich in loam. Fill up the container with the potting soil and then water it well before you plant your carrot seeds.

Use your dibble to create holes for your seeds; each hole should be 6 inches from each other, and each row should be 1 inch apart. Carefully press each seed into the hole in the soil and then cover the hole lightly with soil. Gently water the soil and place your container in an area that gets a lot of natural light, or underneath your artificial light source such as fluorescent lights.

Each day, make sure that the soil is moistened but never soaked. To help keep them moist, you can submerge some peat moss in a pan of water overnight and then layer this on top of the soil the following day.

Your seeds are supposed to start sprouting after 14 days.

Steps to Harvest Them

To check whether your carrots are ready to be harvested, you can carefully remove a bit of soil around the stem of one carrot and check if it is about 3/4 of an inch just below the green stem. Small but ripe carrots taste much better than big ones, so it's alright if you harvest small ones. To harvest each carrot, hold onto the root sturdily and then wiggle it around to loosen it from the soil before you pull it up straight. It will be easier if you water the soil and then let it sit for about 60 minutes before you harvest it. After you have harvested your carrots, wash them thoroughly and cut off the greens before you put them in your fridge.

Potatoes

What's great about potatoes is that they can be stored for extended lengths of time after they are harvested. They can also be grown all throughout the year indoors.

Steps to Grow Them

To plant potatoes indoors, the first step is to purchase seed potatoes that hold plenty of eyes. These are small dots on the potato's skin and it is where the potato will sprout. A potato with at least 6 eyes can produce about 2 pounds of potatoes.

Once you have bought your potatoes, scrub them carefully under running water to get rid of dirt and traces of pesticides. Next, prepare a wide mouth jar that can hold a potato supported by toothpicks on its brim. Fill it up with water.

After that, cut a potato into two pieces without damaging the eyes. Stick 4 toothpicks around the potato, just deep enough for it to support the potato evenly as it will be placed on top of the jar.

Position the potato onto the jar, making sure that the eyes are submerged in the water. Place the jar in a spot that gets a lot of light. Change the water whenever it starts to get murky. Make sure to always keep the eyes submerged.

Once the potato starts to grow roots, you can transplant it to its container. Prepare the container by arranging some pebbles at the base. Make sure that there are drainage holes. Fill up the container with soil, but leave about a third of the container bare, because you will be adding some more soil to the pot as the potatoes continue to grow.

Plant the potatoes with their root side pointing downwards at about 6 inches away from each other. Never plant a potato too close to the edge of the container. After that, cover them with about 2 to 3 inches of soil and water them completely.

After a week, it will start to sprout. When they reach 6 inches above the top soil, add more soil. The moment its vine starts to shoot over the container, create mounds of soil over the plant.

Steps to Harvest Them

You can begin harvesting your potatoes once you notice small tubers on their vines. Dig up the potatoes carefully using your trowel and then lift them out with your hands. Wash them completely before you cook or store them.

Garlic Greens

Garlic is one of the healthiest foods that nature has ever produced. It is even called one of the "super foods" that can greatly improve your blood pressure, cholesterol levels, and lower your risk of developing certain types of cancer and heart disease.

Steps to Grow Them

Growing garlic indoors is not meant for beginners, but growing garlic greens, which you can prepare the same way you do with scallions, is much easier. The first step is to purchase some garlic bulbs that have small cloves. Prepare a container that is 4 inches deep and has drainage holes at its base. Mix some potting soil into the container, leaving half an inch of space between the soil and the container's brim.

Next, you divide the garlic bulbs into separate cloves and make sure not to peel them. After that, you gently push each clove 1 inch deep into the soil, with its pointy end on top. You can bury around 12 cloves in close proximity to each other in the soil. After that, water it well and then position the container in a brightly lit area. Make sure to water your garlic greens regularly for moisture, but avoid soaking them. You will be able to see the garlic greens sprout out after 7 days.

Steps to Harvest Them

You can start clipping off bits of garlic greens for your cooking once they have started growing about 8 to 10 inches long. Keep in mind that the cloves will only be able to sprout out good garlic greens at first, but it won't be as fresh afterward. If you want to have a constant supply of them, you will have to plant some new cloves. Use the old ones as compost for your potting soil.

Salad Greens

Salad greens are your arugula, romaine lettuce, red leaf and iceberg lettuce and they are fairly easy to plant indoors for beginners. They are also very nutritious and filled with vitamins A, C and K along with iron and folate.

Steps to Grow Them

To start planting salad greens indoors, you can buy seeds or starter plants from your nearby nursery or on the Internet. The container must have drainage holes at its base. Fill up the container with some potting soil and then use a dibble or your finger to create holes that are spaced 4 inches from each other.

To plant your seeds, simply sprinkle a few into every hole and then cover it up with some soil. To plant starter plants, gently rub their roots before you plant them into each hole and cover up the space with soil.

After you have planted them, water the soil until it is moistened, but not drenched. Continue to water everyday until you see the sprouts. Once you do, you will need to pull out the weaker looking shoots and keep the largest ones planted. Continue to water regularly.

Steps to Harvest Them

It is very easy to harvest your salad greens. All you have to do is to gently pull off the outer leaves for your personal use. Be careful not to touch the roots so that your plants will continue to grow and produce more foliage.

Microgreens

Microgreens are the "baby" sprouts of your herbs and vegetables, and they are incredibly healthy. A bowl full of microgreens will nourish your body with folate, and vitamins A, C, and K.

Steps to Grow Them

To grow microgreens, you can purchase many different seeds such as those of kale, beets, basil, radishes, Swiss chard, and so on. Prepare a shallow container that is 2 inches deep at most and has drainage holes at its base. Fill it up with potting mix and moisten it with water.

Then, sprinkle your seeds all over the soil, making sure that they are in close proximity but not in contact with each other. Use your sieve to cover the seeds lightly with soil.

Use a misting spray to water the soil and position it in a sunny area with a temperature of about 60 or 70° F. Continue to use the misting spray to water the soil daily; make sure that the soil always stays moist but not soaked.

After 3 to 5 days, you will notice the sprouts coming out. The moment they do, you need to give the microgreens about 12 to 14 hours of light each day. You should also make sure that the soil stays moist but keep the leaves nice and dry.

Steps to Harvest Them

Sprouts that have grown to about 2 inches tall, most likely after 3 weeks, can already be eaten. To harvest them, hold onto the stem and then clip off the leaves with your kitchen scissors. Just make sure not to touch the roots so that the plant will continue to produce more and more. Microgreens can be eaten fresh or kept inside a ziplock back inside your refrigerator for a maximum of 5 days.

Scallions

Scallions are chock full of nutrients that have detoxification and antibacterial properties, much like garlic. They are easy to plant indoors as well.

Steps to Grow Them

To start growing your scallions indoors, purchase a bunch of scallions from the market and then bind the bulbs together with some twine or a rubber band. After that, put them in a glass filled with water up to an inch deep. The water needs to be changed everyday.

After 7 to 10 days, you will notice that baby shoots have started sprouting and the roots have become much longer. Once this has taken place, you may plant the scallions inside a shallow container filled with potting soil. Make sure to water your scallion plant and give it 8 hours of bright light each day.

Steps to Harvest Them

To harvest your scallions for cooking, cut off the green tops whenever you need them. Make sure not to cut beyond 1 to 2 inches of the plant right above the soil. If you want to harvest the white part of the scallion, you can do so once the sprouts are 6 inches long. Carefully extract the root from the soil, then wash them and trim the tops. For storage, you can roll them up inside moist paper towels and then put them in a ziplock bag to be stored in the refrigerator for up to 7 days.

Tomatoes

Tomatoes are actually more of a fruit than a vegetable. However, they would still be a great addition to your indoor "vegetable" garden because they are very delicious and full of lycopene, which is an antioxidant that also has anti-inflammatory properties making it very good for the heart.

Steps to Grow Them

Growing tomatoes requires great patience, so be prepared to wait for a while before you can enjoy their succulent produce. Prepare a pot that is 6 inches deep; this is good for one tomato plant. Fill it up with starter potting mix. After that, bury the seeds about a quarter of an inch deep into the soil. Then water the soil just enough to moisten it but not soak it.

The pot should be placed in a spot that will get a lot of even sunlight. If it only hits one side of the pot, you will need to turn it every so often so that all sides of it will be given light. The tomato seeds will start to sprout after 5 to 10 days.

Once the sprouts are about 3 inches in height, you transplant them from the starter potting mix to potting soil. Give it 14 days after transplanting before you add organic fertilizer to the soil. Make sure to water the soil completely to moisten it, but never to the point of drenching. Once the plant starts to grow taller, you will have to add stakes to keep it vertical and to prevent breakage. Once your tomato plant starts to flower, gently tap the main step and its bigger branches to help promote pollination.

Steps to Harvest Them

Keep in mind that your indoor tomato plants will not bear produce that is as large as those grown outdoors. Nevertheless, your cuter tomatoes will still be delicious if not more so than the larger variety. Tomatoes that can be harvested will look red and feel firm but slightly bouncy when you touch them. You can use a pair of kitchen scissors to clip the fruit from the stems.

Chili Peppers

Chili peppers are a great addition to your indoor garden. They certainly pack a punch and add a lot of hot flavor to your homemade dishes. Chili peppers are actually easier to grow indoors than outdoors, because they thrive in a more controlled environment.

Steps to Grow Them

Beginners can grow dwarf ornamental peppers because they are easier to grow in small containers. Choose a plastic pot container because these can retain moisture better than clay pots. Prepare a plastic pot that has drainage holes and clean it with hot water and soap before filling it with potting soil mixed with vermiculite.

Next, get a handful of chili pepper seeds and

place them flat between damp paper towels to moisturize them. Put this inside a plastic container and close the lid tightly. Then place the container on top of a warm cupboard to help them germinate. After 2 to 5 days, the seeds should be puffed up and ready for planting. You might even see some of them already starting to sprout.

Plant the seeds inside your plastic pot at 2 inches from each other. Then use your sieve to lightly cover the seeds with compost up to about half a centimeter. Lightly spray them with water using your misting spray. Make sure to always keep the soil moist by misting them every so often. The container should be placed in a sunny area, with as much sunlight as possible. Or you can use a fluorescent light and place it about 6 inches over your chili pepper plant. Keep the light on for 14 to 16 hours every day. Keep your plant away from drafts and make sure that the temperature is consistently warm.

Once you see the chili pepper sprouts appear above the top soil, you will need to water them thoroughly until you see the water drain out of the container's base. Feed your chili pepper sprouts with a balanced fertilizer to help them grow strong and yield lots of produce. You can also stake them as they continue to grow.

Steps to Harvest Them

It usually takes 3 months after sprouting for the peppers to be ready for harvest. Make sure to take note of the standard color and size of your chili pepper for you to know the right time to harvest them. Use your kitchen scissors to clip the produce from the stem.

Mushrooms

Mushrooms are delicious and chock full of vitamin C, fiber, and antioxidants. They are also among the easiest crops that you can plant in an indoor garden.

Steps to Grow Them

Beginners can buy a mushroom kit and follow the manufacturer's instructions. Another way to grow them is to prepare a special compost that contains mushroom spawn and place them in a wicker basket. This basket needs to be placed in a dark, cool, and draft-free spot with a temperature of about 60° F. They need to be watered daily.

Steps to Harvest Them

After a few weeks, your mushrooms will start to sprout. You can harvest them once they have reached their optimal size, depending on their variety.

Chapter 13 - How to Grow Herbs Indoors

In this chapter, you will be introduced to the different herbs that you can easily grow indoors.

Basil

Basil is one of the most popular and flavorful herbs that contain anti-inflammatory properties. It can be used in a wide variety of delicious dishes, from pastas and pizzas to pot pies and soups.

Steps to Grow It

Basil thrives in warm climates so make sure to choose a spot where there will be at least 6 hours of direct sunlight daily, otherwise you can use an artificial light. Buy basil seeds or starter plants from your local nursery or on the Internet. Then, prepare a container that is a minimum of 4 inches wide and has drainage holes at its base. Sprinkle the seeds evenly across the soil and cover with a thin layer on top or plant each starter plant in close proximity.

The soil must be fertilized once every 30 days using organic fertilizer such as compost tea. Water at least once a day, particularly whenever the temperature is high. Make sure that the soil always stays moist. You must prune away the top leaves once they start to grow about 6 inches long to promote a thicker foliage. If you see any flowers, you need to remove them as they will make the leaves taste bitter.

Steps to Harvest It

To harvest your needed amount of basil for your cooking, carefully clip a few leaves from the main stem but be careful not to clip off all of the leaves from the plant.

Chives

Chives are a rich source of antioxidants as well as vitamins A and C. They are also easy to plant, whether indoors or out.

Steps to Grow Them

Buy chive seeds at your local nursery or online. After that, prepare a container that is about 6 to 8 inches in diameter. Pour potting mix into it up until it almost reaches the brim of the container. Then, sprinkle the seeds evenly across the soil and then use your sieve to lightly cover the seeds with some more soil for protection. Put the container in a partially shaded area and water it daily. It is important that the soil constantly stays moist.

Steps to Harvest It

Once your chives have started to grow abundantly, you can start cutting the leaves for your cooking. Just make sure not to cut off all of the leaves from the plant.

Cilantro

Cilantro contains a high amount of carotenoids, which is chock full of vitamin A and can help lower your risk of developing certain types of cancer and heart disease.

Steps to Grow It

Coriander seeds are the seed form of cilantro, so you need to look for coriander seeds or starter plants in order to grow cilantro. Prepare a container that is at least 8 inches in depth and has drainage holes at its base. Fill it up with potting soil, but make sure to give a 1 or 2 inch allowance at the top. Gently push each seed into the soil and then water it until it becomes moist.

The next step is to prepare a plastic wrap and cover the top of the container with it. Secure it with some elastic bands. Once the seeds start to sprout and are pushing against the plastic wrap, you can do away with the wrap. The container should be placed in a spot with a lot of light.

Steps to Harvest It

Use a pair of scissors to clip the leaves to

harvest them. Just make sure not to get all of the leaves of a plant.

Ginger

Ginger has a lot of wonderful benefits. It can help minimize inflammation, cure the common cold and sore throat, calm motion sickness and nausea, and it even has antioxidant properties that can help fight certain cancers.

Steps to Grow It

Growing ginger indoors is very easy. All you have to do is to buy a piece of ginger at the local supermarket and then put it on top of moist potting soil in a container, with its greenest buds facing upwards. Put its container somewhere that is partially shaded but still has some sunlight. After a few days, the roots will start to grow roots and the eyes will start to sprout. Make sure to keep the soil constantly moist, but never drenched. Let it get bigger and bigger until you feel that it is ready to harvest.

Steps to Harvest It

Simply pull the entire ginger plant out from the soil and then cut whatever amount you need for cooking. After that, repeat the same processes for how to grow, in order to have a constant supply of the herb.

Mint

Mint is one of the best and freshest herbs to have in your indoor garden. It is tasty and beneficial to your digestive system too. Furthermore, you can prepare fresh mint tea whenever you feel nauseous.

Steps to Grow It

Buy seeds or starter plants from your local nursery. Then, prepare a big and deep pot that is about 10 inches in diameter and then fill it with potting soil. Plant the seeds or the starter plants in the potting soil and then water it until the soil is moist but not soaked. Put the pot in a place that gets a lot of light. Make sure that the soil never goes dry by watering it regularly.

Steps to Harvest It

To harvest some mint from your indoor garden, all you have to do is to clip a bit of leaves from the plant; just make sure not to take all of the leaves from a single plant.

Rosemary

Rosemary is very aromatic and is a very popular herb for roasting. It contains carnosic acid, which is an antioxidant that helps regulate your cholesterol levels and lower the risk of obesity.

Steps to Grow It

Purchase rosemary seeds or cuttings to start off your rosemary plant. Then, prepare a container that has drainage holes at the base. After that, prepare your potting mix, which consists of 2 parts potting soil and one part coarse sand. Add 1 teaspoon of agricultural lime for every 5 inches of potting mix in your container to create an alkaline environment for your rosemary plant. Then plant your seeds or cuttings into the soil and position the container in a spot that is sure to get at least 6 hours of direct light every day. The rosemary plant should only be watered if the top soil becomes dry when you touch it.

Steps to Harvest Them

To harvest your needed amount of rosemary, simply cut some sprigs from the plant. Be careful not to get all of the sprigs from a single plant.

Lemongrass

Lemongrass thrives in an environment that is similar to the subtropics: hot and humid. It is a delicious herb that you can use to stuff your roast or cook with boiled rice.

Steps to Grow Them

Lemongrass needs to get full sunlight at least 8 hours a day, so if you have a spot indoors that can provide that then you will be able to grow it.

Prepare a deep pot that is at least 12 inches deep. Purchase some lemongrass from the local supermarket and place it in a glass that is filled up with just enough water to cover the roots. Make sure to change the water everyday. Once the roots start to grow to twice their length, you can plant the lemongrass to your potting mix. Prepare a moisture-retentive potting mix and water it regularly.

Steps to Harvest Them

To harvest lemongrass, snip a few leaves from the plant, but make sure not to remove all of the leaves, otherwise the lemongrass plant will die.

Oregano

Oregano can grow up to 2 feet high and has beautiful and aromatic round leaves that can sprout up to an inch long. They are often added to pastas, pizzas, meat and vegetable dishes because of their unique flavor and scent. Oregano also contains vitamin A and niacin, and is a great herbal remedy for a stomachache or cough.

Steps to Grow It

Purchase an oregano plant from a local grower center, because it is the easiest way for beginners to ensure a healthy plant that will produce flavorful leaves. Prepare a 12-inch deep and 12-inch wide container (good for one oregano plant), and fill it with well-drained potting soil. Carefully plant the oregano's roots into the soil, and pat the surrounding dirt around its stem to secure it. Then carefully water the soil until it is moist to the touch. Place the container in a spot that gets full sunlight.

Steps to Harvest It

Snip off as many leaves as you need, but never remove all of them from the plant.

Parsley

Parsley can grow up to 12 inches high and wide, and it can produce delicious leaves that are packed with healthy nutrients such as vitamins A and C, iron, calcium and magnesium. It is usually prepared as a pesto mixed with some lemon zest and nuts.

Steps to Grow It

Parsley is an easy herb to grow indoors because it prefers a shady environment. It also likes cool temperatures but it will still need full sun. Purchase parsley seeds and soak them in water overnight before planting them in a wide and deep container at 8 inches apart in a rich and slightly acidic soil. Parsley takes a long time to germinate, so be patient and faithfully water them everyday until you notice the sprouts coming out.

Steps to Harvest Them

You can begin harvesting parsley once it is approximately 8 inches in height. All you have to do is to cut the outside leaves (but avoid cutting off all of them). This will even promote new growth.

Chapter 14 - FAQs

In this section, you will find the answers to the most frequently asked questions about indoor gardening.

Q: If I use artificial lighting, will my electric bill greatly increase?

A: Not as much as you might be thinking. It is, however, important that you check the product details for the average electrical costs on the package of your artificial lighting source. It will usually cost you a lot less compared to a standard household refrigerator.

Q: Is it safe to use MH and HPS lights?

A: A lot of households are actually using MH and HPS lights safely at home. To keep it safe, you can install a smoke alarm in your indoor garden area, and to prepare an automated fire extinguisher in the vicinity as well.

Q: How long do I have to keep the artificial light on?

A: Keep it on for approximately 18 hours and off for 6 hours in order to promote plant growth. As for promoting flowering and fruiting, keep it on for 12 hours and off for another 12 hours. It is recommended for you to use a timer in order to manage your lighting schedule.

Q: What's the difference between a cool bulb from a warm bulb?

A: Cool bulbs are metal halide and emit a white color, while warm bulbs are high pressure sodium and emit an orange or reddish color.

Plants sense the light from cool bulbs similar to spring or early summer sunlight, which is white and bright. This makes cool bulbs, ideal for stimulating healthy plant growth. On the other hand, the warm bulbs emit light that is not unlike mid-summer to fall sunlight, stimulating the production of flowers, fruit or vegetables. Therefore in indoor gardening, it is recommended that you start with the cool bulbs, and then change them to the warm bulbs.

Q: What is Hydroponics?

A: It is the method of growing plants without using soil. Instead, it utilizes a nutrient-water solution. The plants are stabilized by a growing medium and the nutrient-water solution is applied directly onto the root system.

Q: What are the benefits of adopting Hydroponics in an indoor garden?

A: You will be able to grow more plants using Hydroponics compared to potting because there is no need for pots and soil since you will be feeding the roots directly. This makes the roots smaller and allows the plant to focus on growing plant mass instead. It is also noted that Hydroponics makes plants grow faster.

Q: Is Hydroponic gardening high maintenance?

A: Not necessarily. However, it does require you to follow some guidelines in order to successfully apply it.

Conclusion

Thank you again for downloading this book!

I hope this book was able to help you to start your own indoor veggie and herb garden.

Stay inspired to take good care of your plants by keeping a record of your progress on a blog. You can also research some more veggies and herbs that you can easily grow at home and cultivate them as soon as you can.

There are so many benefits when it comes to enjoying fresh produce straight from your own home. As you continue to expand your little indoor garden, you will appreciate the fact that you do not need a wide backyard to enjoy your own homegrown veggies and herbs.

Finally, if you enjoyed this book, please take the time to share your thoughts and post a review on Amazon. It'd be greatly appreciated!

Thank you and good luck!

Made in the USA
San Bernardino, CA
28 July 2015